MAKING PEACE WITH
HUNGER

MAKING PEACE WITH

HUNGER

FOR THOSE TIRED OF
LOSING THE FOOD BATTLE

CELESTE OWENS, Ph.D.

Good Success Publishing
Making Peace with Hunger
© 2019 by Celeste Owens

This book is also available as an ebook.
Visit www.drcelesteowens.com/products.

Requests for information should be addressed to:
Good Success Publishing, P.O. Box 5072, Upper Marlboro, MD 20775

ISBN: 978-0-9978332-7-0 (softcover)

Library of Congress Control Number: 2019901052

This book is printed on acid-free paper. All scripture quotations, unless otherwise indicated, are taken from the New King James Version®. Copyright © 1982 by Thomas Nelson, Inc. Used by permission. All rights reserved.

Front cover image: Maitree Boonkitphuwadon on 123rf.com
Cover design: Adina Cucicov
Interior design: Adina Cucicov

Printed in the United States of America

Dedicated to the memory of Stephanie B. Davis, my rock,
who got me to the second leg of my race.
You'll never be forgotten.

ACKNOWLEDGEMENTS

To Andel: Thank you for being with me through the ups and downs of my health journey. When you vowed for better or worse, you meant it! I love you forever.

To my AJ and Aaliyah: May you always be at peace with hunger knowing God can meet your every need. I love you very much.

To my parents—Pastor Donald and Lady Malinda: What more can I say, but thank you. Your love and encouragement is why I am here today in one peace/piece.

To my siblings—Andrea, Chanelle, Donald Jr., Nicole, Jason, and Stephen: Remember pizza night? Those were the days! I still remember us fighting over who would get Nicole's pepperonis. Thank you all for your support.

To Frank: You suffered a loss at a major cost, but you never lost your faith in Him. Grateful to both you and Brandy

(Stephanie) for your 100% commitment to the advancement of the surrender movement. You'll be my brother always.

To my Kenyan daughters—Maureen, Chelsea, Faith and Abigail: Thank you for your encouragement during our Surrender Fast. I gave up television and this book is the fruit of that sacrifice. I thank God for you every day.

To my Elite 13 Sis-Stars—Chanelle, Chereace, Cherise, Cozzette, Janelle, LaToya, Karen, Nichole, Omiana, Sundra and Tyra: There is no other group with whom I want to do life and ministry. It is an honor to know you.

To Sundra and Jonathan: Who knew our little conversation at a Starbucks would lead to this?! What's next? A college course? Wink.

To the Surrender 365 Ministry Team—Tiffany, Natalie, Shanta, Warren, Karen and Andel: Thank you much for all you to do to advance this Kingdom agenda.

To all my faithful Surrender Break Room Periscopers: Thank you for your support and prayers. Stay surrendered!

CONTENTS

PREFACE

In 2010, I embarked on a journey that would last nearly a decade. I didn't know it then, but through a process of understanding my eating habits and cravings, I would learn to make peace with hunger.

I used to be the biggest junk food junkie out there. I would eat dessert before dinner. Or better yet, instead of dinner. I was completely obsessed with food, especially sugar. I was also completely obsessed with never feeling hunger. So much so, that I would eat in anticipation of getting hungry. Noon would hit hungry or not, I was feeding my belly.

Eating, but rarely feeling nourished.

Eating, but dying physically and spiritually.

A poor diet left my body weak. My blood glucose levels were constantly dropping and spiking. My habits were self-destructive and were leading me down a path to disease.

Then one day, in a moment of clarity, my help arrived in the form of fasting. I surrendered my diet for 40 days. I ate whole foods; nothing processed and no sugar.

I died.

And in the wake of that death a new me emerged; a woman in charge of not only her eating, but her appetites and her cravings.

We were made to crave and this book is about learning how to discipline those cravings so that you can finally live the life you deserve; the life He ordained from the beginning. I pray in the pages of this book, you find the courage to make peace with hunger.

Celeste Owens, Ph.D.
Washington, DC
February 2019

INTRODUCTION

My obsession with food, especially the sugary kind started in the 5th grade. That was the year I learned to fill the God-sized hole in my heart with food.

It was a new classroom and a new group of peers. I was surrounded by children that didn't look like me, talk like me, or accept me. I was not new to the school, having started there in the 3rd grade, but I was new to this group of students.

As part of an integration reform I, along with other children from my neighborhood, were bused to a school and community that were not ready for us. Though we all inhabited the same school building, the administration rebelled against its forced integration by regulating all the black kids to one classroom and the whites to another. For 2 years I had little contact with the white children in the school, but my stellar academic performance won me an upgrade that my little mind was not ready to process. Upon completion of my 4th grade year I was moved to the "advanced" class for 5th grade.

I didn't know what to expect, but what I got was not what I anticipated. I was quickly ostracized for being different. In all fairness my classmates were 10-years-old. Their questions—why is your nose so flat, why is your hair like that, why is your skin dark—were valid questions. Most had never been that close to a black child, but in my 10-year-old head I was different and that was bad.

My "savior" showed up in the form of a girl named Judy (no matter what you're going through, God always sends a Judy). Judy, though white, was also unpopular. She was somewhat overweight, which I assumed contributed to her unpopular status. Whatever the case, I was thrilled to call her friend. She was kind and welcoming, just what an insecure, newbie to the class needed.

There was another girl in our class that to me was the epitome of feminine beauty. Her name was Tina. The one cute boy in our class, Alex, was obsessed with her. They both sat in the row to my left. On any given day, he could be seen rubbing her long hair as she sat in the seat directly in front of him.

I was obsessed with Tina too. She was a porcelain doll with translucent white skin, the tiniest button nose sprinkled with just the right amount of freckles, and long, shiny reddish-brown hair that cascaded down her back. Each day I would sneak peeks at her, hoping she would notice me and also be my friend. I guess in my head, being liked by the pretty girl would make me pretty and lovable too.

In the midst of my obsession came another savior, food. Every Friday was class movie day and every Friday Judy brought me snacks. Our time on Friday (me and food) became my escape from the world. As I watched the movie and secretly ate the snack Judy had provided, usually pumpkin seeds with some type of chewy candy, I left behind all that troubled me about my appearance, my loneliness, and my sense of unworthiness.

From that time period on, food became my go-to comforter. Whether I was going into a new social situation, trying to get through another research project, or unwinding from the day, food was always nearby.

Ironically, as an adult, I had no clue where my obsession originated; I had blocked out most of the negative aspects of the 5th grade and simply thought my eating was just a matter of me liking food way too much.

My turning point came in 2011. I was in the habit of seeking God first thing in the morning. During one such morning, I heard God say, "Stop consuming sugar." I was sure I heard that wrong. I questioned the thought and once I knew it was God, I immediately went into bargaining. *How about I give up sweets during the week? Or just have one sweet treat on the weekend?*

No matter how I bargained the answer remained no. My reaction to that no was one that shocked me. I started to cry uncontrollably. I held my belly and even fell to the floor as I wailed (this is what my sister Nicole later coined the "Cry of Deliverance"). I was in utter distress and didn't think I could go on with life. I literally said out loud, "I am a dead man walking."

Dead man walking?

What was that about? It was entirely inaccurate and a gross exaggeration of my circumstance, but it was how I felt.

So, I took the time to process that one phrase. Let me say here, if you aren't in the habit of challenging your thoughts, I encourage you to make this a daily practice. We are what we think. The Bible tells us, out of the abundance of the heart, the mouth speaks. My mouth had spoken a destructive lie and I was determined to understand why. So, I asked the Holy Spirit and His response was profound:

> Remember the 5th grade? Judy would bring you candy every Friday. It became your escape and from that moment on you associated feeling good with eating junk food. But you are no longer that 10-year-old girl. You no longer need junk food to soothe your emotions. You no longer need to self-medicate with junk food. You just need Me.

Honestly, I wasn't convinced, but it was a compelling explanation. So that February in 2011, I surrendered sugar and embarked on a journey to find peace. The following is a portion of that journey. I hope the content of this book starts a conversation between you and the Holy Spirit. Ask Him to transform you as He has done for me. The journey won't be an easy one, but it will be worth it. Surrender always is.

CHAPTER 1

PEACE WITH HUNGER DEFINED

"I believe then and still do now that how we nourish ourselves is inextricably linked to every aspect of how we live our lives."
—TRACYE MCQUIRTER, AGELESS VEGAN

What does it mean to make peace with hunger? For me, it means not fearing hunger; it means that I willingly allow myself to go hungry in both the natural and soulish realms without panic. It means sacrificing my present comfort in hopes of a future gain. It also means trusting God with my appetites and allowing Him to sanctify them so that they don't destroy me, but can be used for His glory.

The above definition goes beyond food, but it all starts with food. Your relationship with food and the ability to control your appetite will determine how much of your destiny you will fulfill. Think about it. You are what you eat. If you eat the wrong foods, no matter what promises have been made to you in the Bible, they won't be for you. Your food choices play a part in determining the quality and length of your life. Period. Therefore, making peace with hunger and winning the food battle is crucial for the fulfillment of the plan that is on your life.

There was a show on television named Man vs. Food. You may have seen it. Each episode the host was challenged to eat an inordinate amount of food in an effort to "beat" food. Sometimes he won and other times food won. In the spirit realm, the enemy has you on a show called God vs. Food, where your willingness to adhere to God's tailor-made diet for you is tested. Which will win? God or food?

This is not a new concept. Time and time again, individuals and groups of people in the Bible were tested with food. In the wilderness God tested the Israelites' loyalty to Him in this manner. Just a month after their release from slavery they found themselves in the wilderness of Sin. Instead of feeling tremendous gratitude for their newly found freedom, they instead grumbled against Moses and Aaron and made the most absurd claim, "Oh, that we had died by the hand of the Lord in the land of Egypt, when we sat by the pots of meat and when we ate bread to the full! For you have brought us out into this wilderness to kill this whole assembly with hunger." (Exodus 16:3)

In essence they were saying they would prefer slavery to hunger! Their hunger was so powerful that they collectively forgot the miraculous way in which God brought about their deliverance, instead focusing on the temporary needs of the flesh.

God could have easily provided food to them to the full, just as they claimed to have had in Egypt, but He knew He would reveal the condition of their hearts if He temporarily deprived them of it and from that place of lack this truth was revealed: *they did not trust God*. Even as He performed miracle after miracle, manna and quail from heaven, preservation of their clothing and healings, they continued to put their trust in material things rather than Him. God tested them, whether or not they would walk in His instructions, and most of them failed miserably. For that reason, they wandered the desert for 40 years and died, never fulfilling the glorious plan God desired for them. Sadly, their demise started with food.

Even today God continues to test His children with food. Want to know where your heart is with God? Examine your food choices. Ask yourself, "Am I obedient to God in the area of diet? Have I done what God has instructed me to do in this area?" If not, why?

Perhaps these excuses sound familiar:

God told me not to eat _____, but if I just do it in moderation that's okay.

I know I should be eating more fruits and vegetables, but eating healthy is too expensive.

I don't buy fruits and vegetables because they spoil.

> *Fast food is not healthy, but God understands that I don't have time to prepare a meal at home.*

What you are saying in essence is: *God I'm too busy to follow your instructions; I crave food more than you; my hunger beacons and you aren't bigger than it.* And if you aren't careful, that defiance will permeate to other areas of your life. There is a saying that goes "how you do anything is how you do everything." Think about that for a moment and absorb this truth. How you do anything (diet), is how you do everything (ministry, career, relationships, etc.). If you willingly and blatantly disobey God in the area of diet, in what other area(s) of your life are you not allowing God to take the helm?

> *Lord, I know that you want me to stay in my marriage, but I am not happy.*

> *Lord, I know that you want me to love and forgive my sister who has hurt me, but the hurt is too great for me to overlook.*

> *Lord, I know that you want me to pursue my education, but I can't go without an income.*

In other words, "Lord I don't trust you!" So, you make excuse, after excuse to avoid hunger, but all the while you're starving. Your choices and your rebellion are keeping you from being fed by God's best.

Are you getting it? Your food choices can determine the course of your destiny. Not convinced? Read the book of Daniel where he shares his journey of mastering food and subsequently becoming one of the highest officials in the land in which he was a slave. Yes, you read that right, he was a slave. But because his ways pleased God and he was obedient in the area of diet, he witnessed an elevation like no other. Here's his story.

After the capture of the children of Israel by the Babylonians, Daniel found himself in a predicament of grand proportions. Just a teen, he was put in a situation where he had to decide if he would obey God or the King. He and a few of his friends had been chosen by Ashpenaz, the chief of the officials, to serve in the King's court. There he was ordered to learn the literature and language of the Chaldeans. Additionally, the King appointed for them a daily ration from his choice food and from the wine which he drank. Sounds posh, right? Not to Daniel. The Word tells us that Daniel *purposed* in his heart that he would not defile himself with the King's choice food or wine because he had made a vow to God regarding his body and eating.

With that, Daniel and his friends sought special permission to eat the diet God had called them to. It consisted of whole foods: fruits, vegetables, and grains. Permission was granted and for 10 days they ate obediently and at the end of that trial period, they looked healthier and better nourished than any of the young men who ate the royal food. Furthermore, Daniel 1:17 reads, "As for these four young men, God gave them knowledge and skill in all literature and wisdom; and Daniel had understanding in all visions and dreams." Through their obedience, these youth experienced miracles, signs, and wonders and Daniel continued to be promoted in a land in which he was a slave.

Today I believe the "King's choice foods" are the foods that are especially tempting like fried foods, cookies, cakes, candies, sodas and fast food. Because everyone is eating them, we think that gives us an excuse to follow suit, but it is imperative that we purpose in our hearts to obey the Lord. Our obedience will pay handsomely, as it did for Daniel and his friends.

Daniel's story demonstrates that God will test you with food to reveal the condition of your heart and your loyalty to Him. Jesus was also tested in this area. After 40 days of fasting from food and drink in the desert, He was tempted by Satan. The first temptation was...you guessed it, food. Satan, hoping to capitalize on Jesus' hunger, said, "If You are the Son of God, command that these stones become bread." And Jesus answered him, "It is written, 'Man shall not live by bread alone, but by every word that proceeds from the mouth of God.'" (Matthew 4:3-4)

Jesus, though hungry, demonstrated that God was and is bigger than any hunger that we can face. Like Jesus, we must let God decide when and what we eat. Jesus relied on God, not His own miracle powers, for the provision of food. He was willing to obey God even if it meant He remained hungry longer than He wanted to. So we must also obey God.

Are you passing the food test? The same test that has been a major stumbling block for many others in the past? The enemy knows that if he can get you to fear your hunger, he can get you to go against what God has spoken to you about your eating. Whether we are talking about a natural hunger or an emotional hunger, obedience to God is the key to your victory and your elevation.

WHY FOOD?

God wants you fully dependent on Him. Not because He's an egotistical maniac, but because He knows what is best for you, your body, and your future. He is love and everything He does emanates from a place of love, even His directions about your diet. Are you compliant with what He says to eat, how much He says to eat, and when He says to eat? As stated in the last section, in scripture God tested the loyalty of His servants by giving them specific instructions about food.

Why food?

I'm glad you asked. First, I believe He chooses food because it is the most basic primal need of the human, right up there with shelter, sleep and, oxygen. Eating is what we do from the womb and it is what a baby does instinctively. Eating is also one of the few things we get to control. Provided there is enough food available to you, you get to decide what to eat, how much to eat and when to eat. Even babies can control when they eat by simply crying and any mother who has heard the hungry cry, will tell you how quickly it moved her to action. Humans love to feel in control; we love to decide when and how we will do something, especially eating. Once we detect that something is under our control, we are hard-pressed to relinquish that control to anyone else—even God.

Second, having an abundance of food makes us feel safe; while the lack thereof leaves us with a sense of insecurity and danger. It's no wonder that children, who are deprived of food for a certain period of time, hoard food even when food is later available in abundance. I knew a couple who adopted a child and couldn't for the life of them understand why she hid food under the bed when they had plenty downstairs in the kitchen. For that child and others, the threat of going hungry is real, and they never want to go back to that place of vulnerability again.

Indeed, being hungry puts us in a vulnerable position and if you haven't made peace with it, hunger can bring with it feelings of desperation, anxiousness and even depression. When hunger is left unchecked it will cause you to do things that can change the course of your life.

I think you can now see why food is such a big deal. Not only for its ability to nourish, but for what it also represents: power and control.

As I reflect on my life, I can see how food played a major part. It provided security when I was lonely and remained a constant friend. It even became a replacement for God. Yes, I was saved, yes, I prayed, but when I needed emotional comfort and a way to fill the void that was in my heart, food was my first choice.

From 5th grade on to the time I was delivered, nothing comforted and soothed me better than food. When I was happy, I ate; anxious, I ate; lonely, I ate; bored, I ate. The only time food didn't comfort me was when I was sad, then and probably only then would I have no appetite.

As a teen, when I entered a social situation, I was sure to be eating something, like chips or candy. If those things were unavailable, chewing gum would do. No matter what, I made sure to be eating something. Strangely enough, eating in those situations made me feel powerful and successfully distracted me from my social anxiety. Likewise, I was hard-pressed to end the day with some type of candy or other junk food as a way of "unwinding from the day." In this case food gave me a sense of safety and comfort. On into adulthood, food became my all in all; my constant obsession for the emotional voids it filled.

"Thou shalt have no other gods before me" was the first of the Ten Commandments given to the Israelites. Why was this first? That's easy to answer. It's human nature to replace God with something we think gives us some semblance of control. Time and time again, food has proven to be the thing humans put before God.

Take Adam and Eve. They communed with God in the Garden of Eden. They were whole in every way and lived a life of perfection, naked and unashamed, but their appetite would get the best of them. Of all the things the enemy could use to tempt them, he chose food. It was a wise and cunning choice and it worked. His deception is outlined here in Genesis 3:1-7:

Now the serpent was more cunning than any beast of the field which the Lord God had made. And he said to the woman, "Has God indeed said, 'You shall not eat of every tree of the garden'?"

And the woman said to the serpent, "We may eat the fruit of the trees of the garden; but of the fruit of the tree which is in the midst of the garden, God has said, 'You shall not eat it, nor shall you touch it, lest you die.' "

Then the serpent said to the woman, "You will not surely die. For God knows that in the day you eat of it your eyes will be opened, and you will be like God, knowing good and evil."

So when the woman saw that the tree was good for food, that it was pleasant to the eyes, and a tree desirable to make one wise, she took of its fruit and ate. She also gave to her husband with her, and he ate. Then the eyes of both of them were opened, and they knew that they were naked; and they sewed fig leaves together and made themselves coverings.

"Eat and you will be like God." Satan used these words to tempt Adam and Eve to sin and he has used food ever since to tempt us. It's an age-old trick—*if I can get them to be ruled by their belly, I can get them to turn their backs on God, forfeit His promises and abort their destinies.* It's a crafty and diabolical plan and this food game has worked for him time and time again. We think our hunger is the enemy when in fact it is what we allow the enemy to do to satisfy our hunger that is the problem. If you are afraid of hunger, hunger will rule your life.

An example of this is Esau, the first born to Isaac. As the eldest son he was promised certain privileges according to his birthright. He was entitled to double the inheritance of the next born son. It was a coveted position and one that was to be protected at all cost. Yet when he was hungry, his brother convinced him to sell his birthright for a bowl of lentils. Lentils are one of my favorite foods, but it is certainly not worth losing an inheritance. However, there are many people who have sold their birthright; their inheritance from God, for food. Sounds inconceivable? God says "with long life I will satisfy you," yet some cut their lives short with foods they know do not edify their bodies. Some people have made their bellies their God, thus shortening their lifespan and aborting their destiny for a plate of food that will last but a moment.

Our sights should be on the prize and our food choices should line up with the will of God. Esau later regretted his decision to sell his birthright, but the damage had been done; he had sold out for a bowl of lentils. Had he made peace with his hunger, he would have been able to resist the temptation to eat what cost him everything.

MAKE PEACE WITH BEING SET APART

Do you know you are set apart? You are His workmanship, formed in His image, and set apart for His good works. That makes you special, but that truth also requires that you make certain sacrifices. Like it or not, being set apart requires that you surrender even your approach to food and drink. We see it exhibited time and time again in the Bible. There were men and women set apart for His good work, whether they chose to be or not. That might seem unfair, but it is what it is. Making peace with hunger also requires you to release your sense of fair and unfair.

When I first came to learn that God had a restrictive plan for my diet, I spent countless hours comparing my eating habits to the eating habits of others, especially those who were in ministry. *Lord why do they get to eat what they want to eat? Why am I the only one saying no to the unhealthy foods?* It didn't seem fair.

One of the first things I had to learn on this road to peace is that God is just, but He never claimed to be fair. His word says many are called, but few are chosen. Beloved, if you're chosen, get over the idea of fair. It is what it is, so move on.

That's what I had to do, I had to move on and accept that I wasn't released to eat certain things if I wanted to be used fully by God. Like it or not, I was to present my body a living sacrifice, holy and acceptable unto God, which is my reasonable service.

There were others set apart in this way; they, too, were restricted in their food selections. Samson was one, John the Baptist was another. Samson was held to the Nazarite vow as described in Numbers 6:1-21 which means "consecrated" or "separated." The Nazarite vow is taken by individuals who have voluntarily dedicated themselves to God completely.

Samson, a great judge, was a Nazarite from the womb of his mother. As a Nazarite, Samson had to honor three standards: (1) he could not touch a dead body, (2) he could shave the hair on his head, and (3) he could not drink wine, nor touch grapes.

Samson was to be wholly consecrated to the Lord, spirit, soul and body. He couldn't compartmentalize and do some things according to God's will and others as he willed. God needed ALL of Samson to be surrendered to Him and committed to His will.

Like some Christians today, Samson struggled with turning his whole life over to God. He had a weakness: women. But bigger than that was his unwillingness to discipline and subdue his desires in many other areas. It certainly wasn't for lack of help; he had plenty of that. The Word tells us in Judges 13:25a, "And the Spirit of the Lord began to move upon him" which enabled him to do miraculous feats. The problem is Samson didn't call on his help and chose instead to operate in his own strength.

Don't be like Samson. Whatever God is calling you to do in the area of food you can do because of Him. The Word reads, "I can do all things through Christ who strengthens me." Also, in 1 Corinthians 10:13 we are reminded, "No temptation has overtaken you except such as is common to man; but God is faithful, who will not allow you to be tempted beyond what you are able, but with the temptation will also make the way of escape, that you may be able to bear it." Stop trying to operate in your own strength. The enemy is counting on you to fool yourself into thinking you can conquer the food demon on your own. You can't do it; you must put all your dependence on God.

If you aren't careful, like Samson, one weak point will destroy your life. Pretend as you may, we all have a weak point; we all have our kryptonite. What keeps you from succumbing to your kryptonite is prayer and self-control. The enemy of your soul is counting on you not being disciplined in your body. He's counting on you to compromise God's standard to temporarily satisfy your flesh. That's how he got Samson.

Samson's lust for women eventually brought him into captivity; he was tricked by Delilah and it cost him everything. What does this have to do with food? Everything. If you look a few chapters back in the book of Judges, you'll learn that Samson's first test was food and he failed that one too. In Judges 14:5-8, God gave Samson strength to kill a lion with his bare hands. Sometime later Samson was walking along the same road and saw a swarm of bees and honey in the carcass of the lion he had killed. Unwilling to resist the temptation to indulge his sweet tooth (remember he was instructed by God to not touch a dead body), he scooped out the honey with his hands and ate as he went along. He also shared the honey with his parents, not disclosing how he had obtained it. With those actions, Samson demonstrated his rebellious nature. He was saying in effect, God I can choose what I want to eat and what I do. I'm in control.

That defiant attitude started with his food choices and eventually permeated other areas of his life. Author Tracye

McQuirter writes in *Ageless Vegan*, "I believe then and still do now that how we nourish ourselves is inextricably linked to every aspect of how we live our lives." This was true for Samson. His unwillingness to surrender to the will of God cost him a great deal, including his freedom and his eyesight. God in His grace allowed Samson one more feat of greatness, but with that act, he too, lost his life.

Like Samson, some of you were set apart from your mother's womb, chosen for His good pleasure. It may not seem fair that you weren't given a choice of how to live your life, but if you belabor and focus on that point, you will miss the point. More important than a personal choice, is to be chosen by God. God chose Samson from the beginning, and He has chosen you too. Your life is not your own. You don't get to eat what you like? Get over it. In the span of eternity those few morsels of pleasure on the tongue mean nothing. Your destiny is too important to give up for anything. You were chosen by a mighty God to perform great feats on this earth! Won't you surrender all to Him?

MAKE PEACE WITH BEING DIFFERENT

John the Baptist, the cousin of Jesus, was completely devoted to God, even down to his clothing. In Matthew 3:4 it is noted that John's outer garments were made of camel's hair, of which he tied with a leather belt and his food was locust and wild honey. Biblical scholar, John Nolland writes that the decision by the author Matthew to provide a description of

John's clothing and diet shows that both were unusual and worth commenting on.

John was okay being different because he knew his being different was for the advancement of the Kingdom. John wasn't afraid to stand out, to make choices that indicated he was different. John knew he was chosen and set apart for a mighty work.

I used to hate eating differently from everyone else. For one, my stance brought conviction to people and though they didn't always verbalize it, I could tell they were annoyed. I would get the who-do-you-think-you-are-eating-so-healthy looks especially at events that involved food. For a recovering people-pleaser, this was a heavy cross to bear. But I realized very early on, if I couldn't tolerate people's negative opinions regarding my food choices, I would be eaten alive when the real criticism came. This was a matter of acceptance and I had to make peace with the fact that not everyone would accept me.

Second, it would have been okay if I only ate different by the world's standards, but to my disappointment I ate differently by the church's standards too. I had to make peace with hunger rather quickly once I realized I couldn't even eat at church functions. Believe it or not, I went to an event hoping to at least eat the salad and they had put meat in that too! Not organic meat, but processed deli meat that the International Agency for Research on Cancer (IARC) has classified as a carcinogen, something that causes cancer. I think the church missed the memo that when God said be ye separated from the world, He also meant in our diets. Eat like the world, and you're going to die like the world: sick and diseased.

However, for those who choose to obey God in the area of diet, God makes this promise in Exodus 15:26, "If you diligently heed the voice of the Lord your God and do what is right in His sight, give ear to His commandments and keep all His statutes, I will put none of the diseases on you which I have brought on the Egyptians. For I am the Lord who heals you." If you are obeying God's instructions for your body and find yourself diseased, remind your body and your God of this promise, that He will keep disease far from you when you are obedient. If you have given the enemy legal right to your body through disobedience, repent and close that access point.

John's simple food, clothing and lifestyle were visual protest against self-indulgence. John was completely sold out for God and thus willingly tailored his life to fit the call that was on him. John ate locust and wild honey, not because he had to but because he chose to. The pursuit of God and His plan was John's number one goal, everything else could wait.

I'm not suggesting you forego every earthly pleasure, unless directed by God to do so, but there is something to be said for the pursuit of God at all cost. My mother often says, the more you give up for God, the more you show Him how much you want Him and how willing you are to become a vessel for Him. Christians who want to please only their flesh say things like, "it doesn't take all of that." Actually, it does take all of that and so much more.

The Word says, I have been crucified with Christ (Galatians 5:20). The last time I checked, crucified meant death. So, if I rephrase that verse it says, I have died with Christ, my life is not my own, to Him I belong. That also includes what I eat.

I hope you are getting the point by now. Every part of you has to be surrendered to God; nothing should you hold back because it's too hard. For some reason, food often becomes the thing that is too hard for the believer to surrender. But if John could eat bugs and honey (which by the way, may have really been the tree gum from the tamarisk tree, a tasteless, but nutritious liquid) you can eat vegetables, fruit and other healthy foods and not only that, be a mega-force in God's Kingdom. John was. It was said of him by Jesus Himself, "Assuredly, I say to you, among those born of women there has not risen one greater than John the Baptist" (Matthew 11:11a). Do you think John would have gotten that type of praise if he had not first disciplined himself in the area of diet, which then translated to discipline in every area of his life?

By God's grace, you will eat healthier. You will be at peace with your new food choices and not live in a space of regret for what has been left behind. Romans 8:18 reads, "For I consider that the sufferings of this present time (you eating healthy foods) are not worthy to be compared with the glory which shall be revealed in us." Life is about more than just eating, let God's glory be revealed in you by your food choices.

SURRENDER YOUR DIET AND THE REST WILL FOLLOW

I define surrender as doing God's will, His way, all the time. In 2010, when I did my first Surrender Fast, I ate whole foods and no sugar for 40 days. Not because I wanted to, but because it was God's will. Essentially, I did the Daniel Fast for 40 days instead of the standard 21. The Daniel Fast is modeled from the fast Daniel, whom I mentioned earlier, did centuries ago. Mentally, I was nowhere close to Daniel's resolve; he had made up in his mind to not defile his body with the King's delicacies. I was just being obedient to God...I still loved the king's delicacies.

The first 14 days of my Surrender Fast were brutal. My constant prayer was, "God help me to crave and eat the foods that are good for me." I prayed this nonstop because the void that was left by not eating sugar and meat was great. Although I would eat till full, a profound sense of dissatisfaction would hover over my being. I was miserable! Thankfully, somewhere around day 14, I felt my change coming; I actually started to like the foods I was eating and not only that, I felt great. I had gotten through the dark night of my soul; I had challenged my cravings to a dual and won. It was a Christmas miracle. Not in a million years did I ever think I would conquer my sugar demon. I was free (at least for a while, more about that later).

What about meat? Well apparently, meat wasn't for me either. Right about day 28 of my Surrender Fast, I lost all desire to eat meat. I exited the Fast a vegetarian. I often say had I known I would be a vegetarian after my time of fasting I would have eaten a lot more meat prior to starting. Nonetheless, God did a miracle in the area of diet for me in just 40 days. Indeed, some things only come out through prayer and fasting.

Likewise, God has a tailored-made diet plan for you. Stop following every fad diet that comes on the market. Instead fast and allow God to speak to you in the area of diet. Ironically, I'm not eating the way the industry says I should eat. According to the writer of *Eat Right for Your Blood Type*, an O blood type craves and thrives on meat. I'm an O blood type, perhaps God missed the memo. Or better yet, perhaps He knows my body and yours better than man and has an eating plan for our body types that will cause us to thrive and do the good work He has for us to do. Stop living in fear and from your limited vantage point. God knows you and your body best and if He is telling you to eat a certain way, it is for your good. I encourage you to surrender your diet; say goodbye to the foods that don't edify your body and take comfort in the foods that do.

Only God can change your cravings. When I sought him with all my heart, He changed my dietary habits. Interestingly enough, when I allowed him to change my diet, other cravings and desires fell in line with His will too. No longer was I vying for attention from the so-called right people, expecting man to open doors for me. I became content in my desires to succeed, allowing God to order my steps. No longer was I trying to "keep up with the Joneses'" but instead finding contentment in what I had.

This hunger thing is serious and God would rather let you nearly starve than to feed into your every whim. I can recall a time when I was "hungry" for a new home, but for mostly the wrong reasons. Yes, we could use more space for our growing family, but I also wanted a new home for the status of it. I wanted to live in a single-family home, rather than a town-home. I had grown discontent with the gift God had given us in a townhome, instead craving something that I thought would satisfy; something I thought would make me be more successful in the eyes of man. Sure, God wants me happy, but not an artificial, superficial, materialistic happy. His happy includes joy, peace, and contentment. My desire for a new home included none of that. So, He caused me to wait and in that waiting, I learned to be content. I learned to be satisfied in His sufficiency. I made peace with my house hunger.

Then one day out of the blue Andel announced, "We're moving." My first response? "We can't afford to move, besides I am perfectly content living here." However, as I proceeded to climb the stairs to our second level the Holy Spirit whispered, "That is God speaking." He had my attention! I immediately phoned the bank. The first bank told me just what I had predicted: *you can't afford a new home.* Just an aside, you have to be careful what you speak over your life, life just may show up to give you what you declared.

Anyway, I wasn't deterred; I knew Andel had heard from the Lord. The second bank gave me the same answer, but changed their tune when I told them Andel was a veteran. Apparently, those were the magic words that opened the floodgates of opportunity. They told us to go pick out a house; a house, mind you, we moved into within 30 days.

When you are in the flow of God, His plan unfolds right before your eyes. When I satisfied my hunger for material things with Him and started to seek first the Kingdom, all *these things* began to be added unto me. Surrendering my diet translated to me putting under submission all my other desires too. With that God was able to feed me both naturally and emotionally and I was satisfied.

OH SHE GLOWS

There is a website named "Oh She Glows." The day I happened upon it I thought, wouldn't it be cool if the saints glowed? If the saints ate so well, that their countenance reflected the glory of God. It is possible, I am a living witness.

In the last section, we discussed the importance of surrendering our diets to God. I've done this plenty of times. Hands down, the most challenging eating directive from the Lord came in 2015 when He (strongly) suggested I go raw. At that time I thought eating vegetarian was challenging, but now God was suggesting I go raw? God was doing the most!

However, there were some health (prayer) requests I had before the Lord and I realized if I wanted to see the manifestation of those request, I would need to dramatically participate in my own miracle. In other words, if I wanted to see a mighty move of God in my health, I would need to do my part.

One prayer request was the restoration of my knees. Post chemo and post sugar addiction, my knees and joints were in terrible shape; they ached almost every day and it was difficult to navigate stairs or do anything that put pressure on my knees. I was once the squat queen, but at that time I would have been delighted to do 5 good squats. My condition got so bad I was visiting my doctor for bi-weekly cortisone shots and had been diagnosed with rheumatoid arthritis. I was in bad shape and I needed a miracle.

So, without any fanfare or conversation the Lord simply suggested I go raw. It wasn't an audible request, but a directive brought to me by a nudging in my heart and a series of confirmations from other people. The last confirmation came via a conversation I had with my friend Natalie who told me she was considering the Hallelujah Diet. According to their website, the Hallelujah Diet is a plant-based plan that addresses nutritional deficiency, reduces toxicity and improves overall health. Those who adhere to the Hallelujah Diet eat 80 percent raw foods and 20 percent cooked. This group became an invaluable source during my year of eating raw food.

I'll be honest, I wasn't happy about going raw, but for me obedience trumps happiness any day, so with that, on January 1, 2015, I went raw for an entire year!

For the first 3 months of that year, I was 100 percent raw, which meant I only ate raw foods, no meats, no dairy, just raw. Here's a funny story. When my sister Stephanie told my Dad, I had gone raw he exclaimed, "Celeste is eating raw meat?! She has gone too far!" She reminded him that I hadn't eaten meat in 5 years, so eating raw meat wasn't an option. We got a good laugh from that.

At month 4 of my raw food journey, I began to follow the structure of the Hallelujah Diet which incorporates a small amount of cooked food at dinner. I continued in that vein for the remainder of the year.

There were a few remarkable things that came out of my obedience. First, by March of that year I ran a half marathon with my friend Chereace. If you don't know, a half marathon is 13.1 miles. I had only run (and I use that term loosely) a 5K prior to the half marathon. In just a matter of months, I went from being essentially a non-runner to a marathon competitor.

Second, my mood was elevated. Although I probably come across as a pretty happy-go-lucky person, in real life, I have a natural bent towards negative thinking and saddened mood. God, in His wisdom knew that raw food would naturally lift my mood. In fact, about 6-8 weeks into my raw food journey, I begin noticing very strange occurrences in my mood. I would be suddenly joyful for no reason; out of nowhere a wave of joy would wash over me.

After experiencing this a few times, I decided to search the internet for an explanation for my strange mood swings. I found a blog where the writer described his constant feelings of euphoria while on his raw food diet. He equated this elevated mood with the ingestion of foods that had been kissed by the sun and went into his body unaltered. That was an Aha moment for me; God was using raw food to elevate my mood.

Science also confirms the mood elevating effects of fruits and vegetables. According to Australian research that surveyed 12,000 people across a two-year time span, researchers found that with each extra serving of fruits and vegetables people ate, the happier they felt (AJPH, Redzo Mujcic, MD, 2016). This is just one other reason to eat your veggies.

Third, my skin glowed. After about a month or two of being raw, people would stop me to say how great I looked and that my skin glowed. I, too, noticed the marked difference in my skin's tone and texture. I found that I could go without moisturizing creams and still maintain a healthy glow. I also discovered that I could go without deodorant. In general, a clean and balanced vegetarian diet will help you maintain a neutral body odor. The best foods for combating body odor are leafy greens. I was eating plenty of those, so my body was free to smell good, naturally.

That year I was overjoyed to think that I was representing Christ well and I still do. I wasn't sick in my body, I wasn't on any medications and I was eating the food He created. Real food, not the Frankenstein experiments they pass off as food today. Things that can remain on shelves for years without spoiling, or contains high fructose corn syrup, MSG and poisonous colors (e.g., Red 40, Blue 3, Yellow 5, etc.). No, I was eating food and my body reflected my obedience.

What about you? Can people see, by your visual appearance that you are a child of the King? If the answer is no, please know I am not judging you. I'm simply encouraging you to ask the Holy Spirit to strengthen you in your inner being so that you make the changes in your diet that will glorify God. He has a tailored-made diet just for you; all you have to do is ask for it.

The last benefit of going raw came unexpectedly. At the end of 2014, I felt a lump in my breast. It caused me to be a little alarmed, but I quickly reminded myself of my declaration in *The 40-Day Surrender Fast* that I would remain cancer-free in Jesus' name. Therefore, I went about my business in 2015 eating raw food and the lump remained the same size all year. Even my mammogram results indicated it was just calcification. The raw diet kept my cells normal.

However, in 2016 when I gladly abandoned my raw food diet and couldn't stand to eat as much as a salad, the lump grew 3xs the size it had been within 6 months' time and was eventually reported to contain cancer. I have since learned that my body requires lots of fruits and vegetables and no dairy so I have moved to a permanent vegan lifestyle.

Obedience pays handsome dividends. Whatever God is calling you to do in your diet, do it. The sacrifice to go raw was great; I had to prepare my meals ahead of time, especially when eating out or I would be hungry. And, yes, there were times I went hungry, but during that year, like no other, I learned to make peace with hunger. Not just physically, but also in other areas of my life, especially ministry. The hunger to fulfill the promises God had for me at a rapid rate, starved. The hunger to make my name great, starved. God told Abraham in Genesis 12:2, "I will make you a great nation; I will bless you and *make your name great* (emphasis added); and you shall be a blessing." If you are striving to make your name great, stop. That hunger will lead to a starvation death. Wait on the Lord and be of good courage. He has a plan that far exceeds your longing to feed your ego. It is said that ego stands for "Edging God Out." My raw diet got me to a place where I no longer wanted to edge God out. I learned to love people over the promise; I learned to go at the speed and flow of God. Things appeared to move slowly that year, but in 2016 God opened a major door for my ministry and I attribute it to obedience in my diet, learning to manage the ministry hunger and exercising patience as I waited on God's perfect plan to unfold.

PERSONAL REFLECTIONS

1. *Having read Dr. Celeste's definition of "making peace with hunger" how would you define it? What does it mean for you to make peace with hunger?*

2. Currently, what is your relationship with food? At times, do you think you crave it more than God? Though food is necessary for survival we must put all our trust in God. How much of your survival are you willing to surrender to God? How will you prove to God and yourself that He is more important than food?

3. *How does your relationship with food reveal your trust or lack of trust in God? What foods, if any, have God encouraged you to stop eating? Have you or will you cease from eating these foods? List them here:*

4. Dr. Celeste wrote, "If you are afraid of hunger, hunger will rule your life." What does that mean to you? If applicable, how has hunger ruled your life? What one thing do you need to do to demonstrate that hunger/food no longer has or will have control over you?

CHAPTER 2

IT'S NOT JUST ABOUT THE FOOD

"Gluttony is an emotional escape,
a sign something is eating us."

—PETER DEVRIES

Eating for most humans is about much more than nourishment of the body. Often times, the foods we eat have some connection to events in the past and trigger in us certain emotions. The smell of warm apple pie takes you back to your mom's kitchen or a bite of fudge brownie transports you back to middle school having lunch with your friends. Food has the power to do that and it is fun recreating those experiences through food. However, the fun ends when those same foods become not only a trigger for positive emotions, but an addiction that you feel powerless to stop. Having dealt with emotional eating, and at times still dealing with it, I know firsthand how frustrating this cycle can be.

Emotional eating or stress eating is eating to make you feel better; eating to satisfy emotional needs rather than physical hunger. Why do we resort to emotional eating? Because we are emotional beings. There is no way around that, and the key to winning the emotional eating battle is to acknowledge that you are emotional; you have a body that encases a soul and spirit. The soul is the mind, will, and emotions and these emotions will not be ignored.

Because emotional eating is an unconscious attraction towards food used to fill an emotional void, emotional eating usually occurs when one is experiencing intense emotions all at once. Those emotions include, but are not limited to: anxiety, sadness, and depression. Often times in our minds the only viable escape from these negative emotions is food.

It's no coincidence that as adults we use food to feed emotional voids. It all started in childhood. More than likely food was the thing your parents or other caretakers used to soothe, reward, and occupy you. You cried? A bottle was popped into your mouth. You got a scrape on the knee? A lollipop was given for comfort. Bored? A bag of chips and the television became your entertainment.

It's not rocket science to figure out that our parents used food for more than nourishment and in turn as adults, we not only use food to fill our emotional voids, we teach our children to do the same. It's a dangerous cycle that encourages emotional avoidance and eventually affects our overall health and well-being.

WHAT'S EATING YOU?

The United States is in a health dilemma. It is said the rising obesity levels in the U.S. is a public health crisis. The latest federal data shows an increase in obesity rates for adults from 34% in 2007-08 to 40% in 2015-16 (Craig Fryar, MD, *Trends in Obesity*). It is also said that obesity is a public health threat, more serious than the opioid epidemic. It is linked to chronic diseases including Type 2 diabetes, high blood pressure, cardiovascular disease, and cancer. The medical costs of prevention, diagnosis, and treatment are estimated at $147 billion. Unfortunately, despite the thriving U.S. weight-loss market (worth $66 billion in 2017), there is no evidence that diet-related programs will curb obesity.

What's going on? Why are there more diet programs than ever, but Americans are still overweight? Perhaps, making it just about the food is not the answer. Maybe there is another answer; an underlying cause that is not being explored?

If weight gain or loss was simply about how many calories one ingested, everyone would be their ideal weight. Counting calories is easy. In fact, Americans spend countless hours counting calories, and keeping food journals, yet a large portion of our population is obese. I guess it can be said, "What does calories have to do with it?" Indeed, the real problem isn't just what we eat, but what is eating us.

As I wrote earlier, I was once seriously addicted to food, especially sugar. When the time came for me to explore my emotional connection to food, I knew I couldn't do it alone; I cried to God for help. I prayed the prayer, "God show me, me." This simple request was few in words, but big in its impact. Do you know God knows you better than you know yourself? In Jeremiah 33:3, God says cry unto me and I will show you the things you do not know. He also says in Isaiah 58:9, when we seek Him with all our heart, "then you will call, and the Lord will answer."

In matters of overeating, you need God to show you yourself and reveal the underlying reason(s) for your obsession. For me, emotional eating was mostly related to incidences of rejection. For you, it may be something entirely different.

When we overeat, there is a payoff. Some overeat because the feeling of "physical" fullness gives them the illusion that they have also been fed emotionally (that's how I used food). Others see weight gain as a payoff for overeating. Often, from an unconscious level, people sabotage their dieting efforts because deep down they use their fat as a security blanket. They see fat as a way for them to keep people at bay, especially in romantic relationships.

For a decade, I worked with survivors of childhood sexual abuse. I learned that some of them gained weight as a way of keeping people out; the weight was literally their wall of protection. In his book, *The Body Keeps the Score*, Bessel van der Kolk, MD, shares a story of a woman who went from 405 lbs to 132 lbs in one year then gained half the weight back in 3 months after a co-worker showed a romantic interest in her. She later disclosed to Dr. van der Kolk that she had been the victim of repeated raped by her grandfather. The weight had become her protection and her defense.

With that in mind, could it be that overeating and/or being overweight is more an emotional issue than a discipline issue? Perhaps now some of you can let yourself off the hook. Rather than shaming yourself for eating too much, let God help you root out what is eating you. Romans 8:1 tells us, "There is therefore now no condemnation to those who are in Christ Jesus, who do not walk according to the flesh, but according to the Spirit." There is no condemnation in Christ; He is not judging you, but lovingly drawing you to Him for your complete healing. He loves you and has no desire to shame you. Because of His love, He wants you to get to the bottom of your eating problem and live the abundant life He promised.

Acknowledgement is huge. It is said that you are halfway to resolving your issue by simply acknowledging a problem exist. Once you acknowledge you have an eating problem, you can then make steps toward resolving it. Don't do this on your own; seek God's wisdom, tell a trusted friend and/or seek out a good Christian counselor.

Lastly, what would your excess pounds say if they could speak? How might God direct you in the area of diet, if you turned this over to Him? God wants you to lay the weight you carry at the feet of Jesus. Cast your cares on Him, His yoke is easy and His burdens are light. His word says, "Come unto me all who are heavy laden and I will give you rest." You can find rest in this area, just as I did. The thing that is eating you can be a thing of the pass. Just surrender all to Him.

That's how I found the root to my sugar addiction. I asked God; I cried out to Him for help. His first instruction was to stop eating in bed. That was not what I was expecting. I wasn't expecting a directive; I just wanted to know the why. But I guess God knew, at that moment, I couldn't handle the truth. So instead, He instructed me to eliminate a certain behavior. As a matter of fact, it would be another year before I uncovered the whole Judy story.

So again, God's first instruction was to stop eating in bed. On the surface that might sound like a reasonable request, maybe even easy, but for me it was WWIII. God was asking for a fight. Why? Because eating in bed was my most favorite pastime. All of my best, most indulgent eating happened in my bed, but it wasn't all I chalked it up to be. Night...sugar... shame, that's pretty much how it went and no matter how many times in the morning I declared, "no more," I was powerless to the draw of sugar. So, when God said no more eating in the bed, I knew why. He wanted me free.

Interestingly enough, this directive was probably just as much to help Andel as it was to save me. When I was living the single life, the crumbs from cookies and wrappers only affected me, but as a married woman my crumbs also affected my husband. He would occasionally ask, "Why are there crumbs in the bed?" I would give him the you-better-mind-your-business-look. Was he really worrying about a few crumbs? I do recall making vows that declared we were in this thing for better or for worse. If crumbs were the worse he was going to get, he should count his blessings.

All joking aside, my eating in bed was an indication of a bigger problem that God was urging me to face head on. It wasn't easy. At first all of my focus was on how much I wanted to eat in bed and how much I missed the pleasure it brought me. Then eventually my attention turned to why eating in bed was such a draw for me. In my time of reflection, I learned, that not only was it a way for me to unwind from the day, it also made me feel safe, secure, and loved. A full belly always represented those things for me, but God in His infinite wisdom desired that I find love, security and safety in Him. My substitute food god would eventually lead me to poor health and possibly a shortened lifespan, but putting all my trust and hope in Him, would allow me to live my best life.

It took some time, and a few backslides but eventually eating in the bed became a thing that no longer had the same draw. I had mastered it and that felt great.

PIZZA NIGHT

A key to overcoming emotional eating is to reflect on how food was used as comfort. Begin to understand at what times and with what occasions did food make you feel good. Understanding this will allow you to stop recreating these positive feelings and experiences with food alone.

Growing up, pizza was used as a reward for accomplishing a task. For example, my Dad was an associate minister at the Deliverance Temple, C.O.G.I.C. As a minister, he was expected to deliver a sermon at least once a month. On the Friday nights that it was announced my Dad would be the speaker (they often didn't get advanced notice) we would get super excited. Not because we were hungry for the word of God that would pour from my Dad's lips, but because of the reward that sermon would bring: an offering. With that offering my Dad would buy us pizza. In a city like Buffalo, which has the best pizza on the planet, we gladly enjoyed every morsel of my Dad's accomplishment in the form of pepperoni pizza.

To this day my favorite food is pizza, hands down. For me pizza still represents satisfaction, happiness and accomplishment. For that reason, every Friday night in our home is pizza night, though only my daughter still eats it. To my disappointment, both my husband and son tired of the tradition a few years in. Ironically, I was forced out of the tradition, ever so slowly through God's direction. The first transition came in 2010 when God directed me to go vegetarian. It took months for me to make peace with losing my pepperonis, but nonetheless pepperoni or no pepperoni, pizza continued to be my favorite food; not only for the taste, but for how it fueled my emotions.

Imagine my shock when God told me to go raw. How was I to conjure up satisfaction, happiness, and accomplishment with raw pizza? I tried, but it was an epic fail. Raw pizza is just *not* okay. (Sorry raw food enthusiast!) I missed pizza, in a major way, the entire year of 2015. I scrambled to make it a food staple once my raw year ended.

However, in 2015 my affair with pizza was in its last days. For my health's sake, God instructed me to eliminate dairy (some research has found a correlation between dairy and breast cancer). In fact, I had felt that nudging from the time I went vegetarian, but ignored it. With this new directive, I was panicky. No cheese? No pizza? It took me 3 more years to finally go vegan for good.

Fortunately, pizza night no longer has the same pull; my Friday night transport back in time through pizza has ended. I've now learned to enjoy the satisfaction of ending a week, without the need for pizza to punctuate its ending. Believe it or not, I can still conjure up feelings of accomplishment and happiness without pizza. All I have to do is feel the feeling.

You, too, can get the positive feelings you want without the food prompt (particularly if those foods are bad for your health). One technique I use to weaken food's hold on me is gratitude. Gratitude allows me to celebrate the present, which in turn, magnifies positive emotions. Gratitude is a great replacement for whatever area food holds you hostage. At the end of the week I take a moment to thank God for a good, productive week and then I just allow happiness and satisfaction to engulf me. It's that simple. Gratitude doesn't sabotage your health goals, but instead allows you to live in a state of wholeness where you have the power to put food in its proper place.

COFFEE WITH MAMA WILLIE

I can see her now, my grandmother, at the stove watching the pot for the first sign that the water it contained was hot enough for her morning cup of coffee. Upon boiling, she would promptly remove the pot from the stove, walk over to the kitchen table and pour the water over her tablespoon of Sanka instant coffee. She would then drop in a few spoonfuls of sugar, pour in the cream, stir and taste. It was always perfect. How do I know? I was her coffee buddy. She would always share a saucer full with me and that's how we spent our Saturday morning, her sipping from her cup and me sipping from my saucer.

My grandmother died when I was sixteen, but my love of coffee remained alive and well. Even in my twenties, when I discovered that caffeine gave me headaches, my affair with coffee would not end. I just switched to decaf.

For years, I would have Saturday morning coffee with my children. We would go through the same ritual of sitting at the kitchen table, preparing the coffee (although now it was in a Keurig), adding the cream and sugar, and then sipping as we smiled and enjoyed one another's company. I was surprised by people's negative reaction to me serving my kid's coffee. "It's decaf" was always my response. In hindsight, I guess our behavior was a little unorthodox, but had they had a Mama Willie in their childhood, they would have understood completely. In my world, coffee conjured up feelings of belonging and being loved.

Not too long ago, while visiting Costa Rica, I had the privilege of watching how they made coffee. After the demonstration we were served fresh brewed coffee. With one sip I was instantly catapulted to my Mama Willie's kitchen. It was absolutely amazing. I shared my travel back in time moment with Andel, but he didn't quite get why I was so excited. We drank the same coffee in Costa Rica, but his experience was entirely different. That's the power of food.

I never consciously connected my love of coffee with my morning ritual with my grandmother until writing this book. And perhaps now, with this epiphany, I can let go of the decaf once and for all (*they* say decaf isn't good for my health. I wish *they* would mind their business).

CHEWY CANDY

You've already read how I developed a love affair with chewy candy like Swedish Fish, Sour Cherries, and Hot Tamales. Each Friday Judy would bring these types of candy to class along with pumpkin seeds all of which were contained in a brown paper bag. From then on nothing brought me comfort like chewy candy. For me chewy candy represented love and being cared for.

That's why as an adult, and to my chagrin, I ate just as much, if not more chewy candy then I did as a child. I would go to the big food warehouses and buy the bulk size container. You know the one that was supposed to last me months instead of the week it took me to devour it. Yes, that one. I couldn't get enough of it. I stored it in my purse, in my nightstand, and anywhere else needed for quick access.

Funny thing is that like I did in the 5th grade, I still ate my candy in secrecy, not wanting to be found out by the "teacher" and punished. When I became a mom, I vowed I would stop eating candy in order to be a good example to my children, but who was I fooling? Without missing a beat, I continued my affair with chewy candy. My kids would often say, "Mom, what are you eating" and I would remind them to mind their business. It was all really sad.

My turning point came in 2011 when God directed me to stop consuming sugar. By His grace, I successfully completed that year without consuming cookies, cakes, and candy. It was challenging at first. Every time I saw Swedish Fish at the grocery store my mouth would water like Pavlov's dog, but eventually it got easier. The following year at Thanksgiving I convinced myself that I was over the sugar-thing and could consume the holiday desserts in "moderation." It wasn't until January of 2013 that I came to myself; ashamed and 7-10 pounds heavier. That sugar binge taught me that I couldn't moderate sugar, but had to remove it from my diet completely.

MASTER YOUR FOOD TRIGGERS

I share these stories to say, it's important to identify your food triggers; to learn what foods are tied to which emotions and master that area of your life. This is crucial for your overall physical and emotional health. Why? Because if you don't master your dependence on food you will simply find other ways to feed your emotions when that food item is unavailable. This is witnessed with some individuals who have had weight loss surgery and can't consume as many calories as they once had. Rather than find freedom and happiness in their newfound shrunken body, they find other ways to "feed" their emotions through replacement vices. That's also the draw of a diet; it gives you an outlet for your emotions, a distraction, a way to temporarily take command of your cravings. Notice I used the word *temporarily*. Many people are using a temporary solution—counting points, watching calories, eliminating certain food groups—for a problem that needs a permanent fix. These weight loss techniques aren't bad in and of themselves, but if they are just a distraction from the real issue, they serve no purpose. God wants you delivered; He wants you to get to the heart of the matter and find victory in Him.

If food has control over you, take the next few minutes to identify which foods are the worst offenders. Ask yourself why these foods might be so important to you. Travel back to your childhood, how were these foods used for comfort? If food was scarce, ask yourself are you now using food to signify abundance. We all have a food story, it's time to master yours and find greater fulfillment in God.

MY DETOX IN THE WILDERNESS

At birth I was complete in every way, but being born into a sinful world brought me face-to-face with an enemy that sought to destroy me. That enemy was rejection. To this day it is still my kryptonite and for some pretty powerful reasons.

Did you know that rejection piggybacks on physical pain pathways in the brain? It's true. Functional Magnetic Resonance Imaging or Functional MRI (fMRI) studies show that the same areas of the brain become activated when we experience rejection as when we experience physical pain. This is why rejection hurts so much (neurologically speaking). In fact, our brains respond so similarly to rejection and physical pain that it is said that Tylenol can reduce the emotional pain rejection elicits.

It's no wonder that once experienced in my youth, rejection made me hungry. Not in the natural, but emotionally and spiritually. Unable to decipher between the natural and spiritual hunger, I attempted to use natural means to feed the spiritual deficit. It was a futile effort; I was hungry on the inside and an outside solution would never do. Nonetheless, for years I convinced myself food was my answer.

So rather than deal with my emotional hunger, I focused on my natural hunger. I was sure to never be hungry; at breakfast I was planning what to eat for lunch and as I was eating lunch, I was planning what would be my dinner and of course plenty of snacks in between.

The only time my plan-for-the-next-meal-while-you-are-eating-the current-meal didn't come into play was when I was dieting, which I did a lot of. There was something about starving myself that gave me a sense of control over my body and emotions. There was the cabbage diet, the Atkins diet, and the only-eat-canned-corn-diet (I made that one up). You name it, I did it. I thought my dieting was about the weight, but it was really about managing my emotional hunger and staying in control of its desire to be acknowledged at all times. And when starving myself became too much to bear, I binged. Always in a cycle of feast to famine. Never in a space of balance and wholeness.

For a long time, I ran from my emotional hunger; I feared it. In fact, I didn't even acknowledge it because I had found a way to avoid its hunger pains. An avoidance that led to me substituting my healing for the temporary comfort food provided. I made binging about my physical cravings, "I have a taste for..." and while that was true to some extent, what I really needed to do in those moments was to do a soul search and understand what emotion was driving the craving.

You may not realize this, but wilderness experiences will bring every emotional craving to the surface. Today we don't literally go into the wilderness as the children of Israel did, but God will lead us to our own personal wilderness experiences to test our loyalties to Him. God forces us to come face-to-face with our demons, our longings, and the part of our being that has been deprived of Him for too long. So, when the time was right, God tested me in this area. Not to frighten me, but to bring me to a place of wholeness.

My wilderness was Chicago. It was at a crucial time in my life, the final phase of my Doctoral program and my first year of marriage. Don't get me wrong, living apart for our first year had its advantages; we felt as if we were on a year-long honeymoon, each weekend used productively as we spent quality time together. But living apart also had its disadvantages, one being that I didn't know what to do with the loneliness I felt day in and day out, as I lived in a city and with people that were foreign to me. Sounds a lot like my 5th grade, right?

I had felt this type of loneliness just years before in Baltimore, my other wilderness. No friends plus no family equaled LONE-LY. Not a normal lonely, but the type of lonely that feels as if it has taken on physical form and clings to you as its life source. I didn't pass the loneliness test in Baltimore and God had given me a do-over in Chicago.

I wish I could say I passed the wilderness test the second time around, but I can't. In Chicago, I repeated the same patterns I had in Baltimore. I guess I'm a slow learner. However, what I learned to do in Chicago that I hadn't done in Baltimore was to start the day with the reading of God's Word. Until this day that is how I start my morning.

What I hadn't mastered in both Baltimore and Chicago was a way to unwind from the day. After a long day of listening and providing counseling to children and adult survivors of trauma, I was emotionally spent. I had nothing left to deal with my feelings of loneliness, so I turned to food for comfort. I would stop at the grocery store, just blocks from my apartment, and buy my typical feast: frozen pizza, chips, preferably salt and vinegar, some type of chewy candy, and a 2 liter of red soda (these each have their own food trigger story I won't get into here, two were discussed earlier in this chapter). Then eat myself into a food coma. With this, the loneliness was effectively ignored, but the shame that was left from eating nearly 2000 calories in one sitting was equally unbearable.

I was in a vicious overeating cycle that I didn't know how to stop and was unwilling to allow the Holy Spirit to show me a more excellent way. In some strange way I was okay with my raggedy choices; I hadn't reached bottom, so I was willing to keep on falling. It would be years before I was gently "forced" to look at my eating habits and their powerful connection to my emotional hunger.

What emotions have you not dealt with or faced? This would be a good time to reflect on your eating habits and invite the Holy Spirit to shed some light on how they may be connected to negative emotions you have yet to deal with. Jeremiah 33:3 tells us that God will show you the "fenced in things," that is, He will give you great insight.

One of my favorite prayers is "God show me, me." With this, I give Him permission to search my heart and shed light on the areas that are in need of healing. Warning. Be ready for the onslaught. If you pray this prayer sincerely, the Lord will truly show you yourself and oftentimes it is not pretty.

I pray this prayer often, and God in His faithfulness shows me myself and from that place of insight, I am able to grow. If you, too, want to grow, pray this prayer concerning your eating habits. God wants to help you gain control over your eating and your appetites so that you learn to turn all your hunger over to Him.

PERSONAL REFLECTIONS

1. *What foods do you crave when you are experiencing negative emotions?*

2. *Dr. Celeste wrote that the key to overcoming emotional eating is to reflect on how food was used as comfort in your family of origin. What foods did your parents use to make you feel good or which foods are attached to positive experiences? Has God called you to stop eating those foods? With this new insight, will you surrender that food item for good? If yes, set a date in the near future and don't eat that item after the date you set.*

3. *We all have a food story. If food has control over you, take the next few minutes to identify which foods are the worst offenders. Ask yourself why these foods might be so important to you. Travel back to your childhood, how were these foods used for comfort? If food was scarce, ask yourself are you now using food to signify abundance.*

4. *If you are overweight, does your fat have a purpose? What purpose is it serving?*

5. *What emotions have you not dealt with or faced?*
   Meditate on Jeremiah 33:3, ask God to give you great
   insight so that you can effectively deal with these emo-
   tions without the assistance of food.

6. Dr. Celeste said that instead of food, she uses gratitude as a way of conjuring up positive emotions. Try this exercise for a week. When you are feeling the emotional pull to eat, write down 3 things you are grateful for. During this exercise it's important that you feel the feeling attached to your gratitude statement. Work on recreating the feelings with gratitude instead of food.

CHAPTER 3

WHOSE GOD IS THEIR APPETITE

> "Food is not your God,
> so stop paying homage to it."
> —DR. CELESTE OWENS

Appetite, as defined by Merriam-Webster Dictionary is an inherent craving or the desire to eat. Another way to look at appetite comes from the Bible in Philippians 3:19 which reads, "Whose end is destruction, whose god is their belly, and whose glory is in their shame—who set their mind on earthly things." Other translations read, "Whose god is their appetite." In this scripture, appetite is a deep self-centeredness where the desires come first.

Sadly, we have become slaves to our appetites. What we want, we eat with little to no acknowledgement or direction from God. I was there. After my traumatizing 5th grade year of school, food became a constant in my life; my obsession.

Being a hostage to food is an easy addiction to maintain. Food is everywhere as we all must eat to live. So, for me I was able to rationalize my overeating by convincing myself it was something I needed to do anyway. So what I wasn't hungry? It's wasn't a big deal.

Or was it? The enemy of your soul is counting on you rationalizing your overeating; he wants to use your ignorance in his plan to destroy you. The Bible tells us the enemy comes not but to steal, kill and destroy. He cares not what method of destruction you choose, he just wants to do you in. Notice I said what method of destruction *you* choose. He can't destroy you without your cooperation.

His plan to destroy us with food is so diabolical that he has infiltrated our food supply. When the Bible refers to wickedness in places, I wonder was God referring to the US Food and Drug Administration (FDA). The agency supposedly in charge of approving what is good and acceptable to eat. Don't be fooled, the FDA is not for you, nor the pharmaceutical companies for that matter. The devil has infiltrated these systems and has a plan to destroy you through your ignorance.

Food nourishes and food kills. Shouldn't be able to write that in the same sentence, but it is true. The devil had a plan to destroy me through my food choices. He knew I was too "holy" to be deceived by his other devices like drugs, alcohol, suicide, etc. Those schemes wouldn't fly with me, but because I had not sanctified my appetite and was looking to fill my emotional needs with food, he knew he could get me in this area.

And get me he did!

To the tune of cancer. I was diagnosed with breast cancer in 2007. At that time, I was one of the worst eaters on the planet. I was eating dessert with every meal, and sometimes eating dessert instead of the meal. No matter how many times the Holy Spirit told me to stop, I wouldn't listen. I would use excuses like, *it's just a little slice of cake, everyone else is eating it,* or *it's okay as longs as I am doing it in moderation.*

Let's pause here. Is there really such a thing as moderation when it comes to sugar? No, there is not. Our brains have no mechanism to shut off our intake of sugar; there is no satiation point. That's why you can eat broccoli and stop when you are full, but eat an Oreo, then another until the whole row is finished and even then feel as if you can go into the second row.

Sugar, the white, refined sugar that looks like cocaine, is from the devil. It is his weapon of choice because the saints use it for reasons that have nothing to do with nourishment. Sadly, sugar is acceptable in the church, even pushed. I can recall when I first stopped eating sugar in 2011, I said to one of the saints at a church event, mind you, "I don't eat sugar." Do you know she insisted I try it anyway? "Just a little taste, it's so good." I was tempted, but the Bible promises that no temptation has come upon us that He doesn't provide a way of escape. His way of escape that night for me was discipline. I had to literally run from the sugar-pusher. You will need to do that too. RUN, they are everywhere. Even places you wouldn't expect like the bank and the shoe store. In fact, my bank has cookies right at the front door when you walk in. It's nearly impossible to escape the sugar demon.

Joyce Meyer tells a story that may change your approach to random dessert eating. She said she only allows herself to have one dessert a week, I think it's on Sunday. So even if she goes to the shoe store on Monday and they are handing out cookies like coupons, she says no because it is not her dessert day. She has learned to master her appetite and obey God in the process. Now that is discipline.

Learning to discipline yourself in the area of food will translate to discipline in so many other areas of your life too. Once I learned to say no to sugar, no to other things, like the wrong opportunities didn't seem so hard.

However, mastering the sugar thing is no joke. It's everywhere! Even in foods you wouldn't expect to find it. That's why it is time to return to basics. To cook like our foremothers; cooking whole foods that edify the body. You say you don't have time? There are 24 hours in a day. Eight of those are for sleep. With the 16 hours that are left you must find the time to prepare or purchase a meal that will add to your life, not detract from it. Your health and what you eat must be a priority. Your destiny depends on it.

There are many dreams that God has placed in my heart. Some have come to pass, while others tarry until the appropriate time. Although those dreams are God's desire for me, the fulfillment of those dreams in part depend on me; I must do my part. God has said I will have my own airplane. That tells me that my travel will be so frequent I will need a faster, more convenient mode of transport. However, if I don't properly care for the temple/body God has given me, private jets will be unnecessary as most of my time will be spent in my doctor's office.

Some of you have dreams to leave your children an inheritance, but the achievement of that dream can't be at the expense of your health. Working overtime, driving yourself into the ground and eating what is convenient, is a recipe for disaster. With so many young and middle-aged adults caring for their aging parents, I think the best inheritance you can leave your children is their freedom. Don't have them caring for you at the end of your life because you neglected to eat and care for your body properly.

If you are going to live out God's will, you must make your health a priority. The food items you're hungry for, that don't edify your body, ask God to take the desire to eat them away from you. It takes courage to say a prayer like that; to willingly ask God to remove the food(s) that have been your emotional life source. However, in praying deliverance from these foods, you are giving God permission to be your all in all; your everything.

As I mentioned in Chapter 1, I prayed this type of prayer continuously while doing my first 40-Day Surrender Fast. It wasn't called a Surrender Fast then, but surrender was what I was doing. For 40 days I surrendered my diet and committed to eating only whole foods and that fast radically changed my approach to food. Today I eat a plant-based diet, and no refined sugars; just foods that edify my body. Thankfully, my appetite is no longer my god; He is. I am obedient to Him and Him alone. Now I am living the life He planned from the beginning.

IT RUNS IN MY FAMILY

There are many sacrifices I've made for my health's sake. While I'm not perfect in my diet, I do my best to honor my temple in a way that pleases God. Where are you in your health? This is not a novel concept, but it stands to be repeated. If you want to be healthier, you must stop eating the foods that keep you from achieving that goal. You say you want God to heal you, but are you willing to do your part?

Bottom line, if you have been diagnosed with a disease there are certain foods you will need to eliminate from your diet and other foods you'll need to add. The foods you must add are probably foods you have no desire to eat. I know it doesn't sound fun and you would rather God heal you miraculously with His magic wand, but you must participate in your own miracle. When I first started this healthy eating journey, I didn't enjoy the foods right away, but as my palette became accustomed to my new diet, I started to enjoy the healthier foods.

A few years ago, when Andel was diagnosed with both hypertension and Type 2 diabetes, he was devastated. Although he has a history of both diseases in his family, he knew there were certain dietary patterns he had followed that contributed to these diagnoses. Some people act as if a family history of a disease dooms them to have it too. That's simply not true. If you have a family history of diabetes, your own risk may increase, but that doesn't mean you have to get it. If you were doomed to get it that would make God a liar. He promised, "If you diligently heed the voice of the Lord your God and do what is right in His sight, give ear to His commandments and keep all His statutes, I will put none of the diseases on you which I have brought on the Egyptians. For I am the Lord who heals you" (Exodus 15:26). God keeps you well and heals you when you diligently heed His voice and do what is right in His sight. You're walking around here diseased, blaming it on "family history" when you've done none of what God has required. You're not diseased because of your grandfather, you're diseased from your own disobedience.

Andel knew his health was his responsibility, so he did some things to reverse the diagnoses. One, he repented. Repent means to not only say I'm sorry, but to turn from your wicked way. Two, he prayed for God's healing and the strength to do his part. Three, he increased his cardio workouts at the gym. Four, he incorporated essential oils like Ylang, Ylang and Cinnamon Bark that lowered his blood pressure and regulated his blood sugar levels. Lastly, he changed his diet. He took foods out of his diet that contributed to poor health and added the foods that benefited his health. Right there is where I may have lost half of you. Unfortunately, some of you are like the Rich Young Ruler in Mark 10:18-27 who asked Jesus,

"Good Teacher, what shall I do to inherit eternal life?" And Jesus said to him, "Why do you call Me good? No one is good except God alone. You know the commandments, 'Do not murder, Do not commit adultery, Do not steal, Do not bear false witness, Do not defraud, Honor your father and mother.'" And he said to Him, "Teacher, I have kept all these things from my youth up." Looking at him, Jesus felt a love for him and said to him, "One thing you lack: go and sell all you possess and give to the poor, and you will have treasure in heaven; and come, follow Me." But at these words he was saddened, and he went away grieving, for he was one who owned much property.

As Jesus listed the requirements, the young man must have been quite pleased with himself as he had done them all. However, when Jesus said in love, "sell all you possess and give it to the poor," the young ruler left saddened because he owned much property and was unwilling to part with his possessions. This exchange is less about the things and more about the condition of his heart which loved his things more than Jesus.

Which do you love more, your food or Jesus?

It's a very important question. If you cannot answer "Jesus" with all certainty it's because you have made your belly your God and if you aren't careful your appetite will kill you. Andel changed his diet, not because he wanted to, but because he valued his life as much as God does. And because God thought he was worth saving, Andel did his part to save himself. Then within 3 months' time, every symptom of disease was reversed and he came off all medications. His faith and obedience made him whole.

What do you need to do to be healthier? Make a list and one by one do your part. You don't even have to do a whole lot of research about your ailments, just ask the Holy Spirit what you should do. I promise you He will reveal the perfect plan for your wellness. He did for me.

In 2007 I was diagnosed with Stage 3c breast cancer. It was an aggressive form of cancer that the doctor's believed had traveled to other parts of my body. Thankfully, God healed me. For 3 years post-treatment the Holy Spirit urged me to change my diet. I finally complied in 2010 and since that time I have embraced a full wellness lifestyle which consists of prayer, meditation, healthy eating, supplements, essential oils and exercise. I didn't learn until post cancer that the side effects of chemotherapy drugs can last for up to 7 years. For that reason, God placed me on a healing plan that included supplements, detoxing of the body, cleansing of the blood, and dietary change. I didn't know why God was calling me to do certain things (like eliminate meat and sugar), I was just following along in obedience.

In 2014, my sister Stephanie and I became Certified Natural Health Professionals. During our intensive week-long training I learned some things that blew me away. One of the instructors mentioned the long-lasting side effects of chemotherapy. He then listed the things one must do to get back to good health: remove meat from your diet, eliminate white, refined sugar, do a full body detox, cleanse your blood, incorporate supplements like a multivitamin and digestive enzymes, and drink lots of water. I hit my sister and gestured to her that I was already doing all of that. God is amazing; He knew what my body needed to heal itself and He knows what your body needs too. He says in His word, "Trust in the Lord with all your heart, and lean not on your own understanding; in all your ways acknowledge Him, and He shall direct your paths." (Proverbs 3:5-6)

You want to be in your best health? Acknowledge Him and He will make your crooked path (family history of disease) straight. He did it for me in the area of cardiovascular disease.

Heart disease runs in my family. My dad's mother had a heart attack and died at the age of 42. My dad had his first heart attack at 42. Erroneously, I thought they both had heart attacks at 40, so for my entire 40th year I held my breath. I finally exhaled at 41. With that exhale, I phoned my dad, proud that I had made it past the family curse. "Da, I'm 41. I made it. I didn't have a heart attack." His response, "We had heart attacks at 42." I was done. There was no way I was going to hold my breath another year. I turned my worry over to God and have had no heart conditions since that time. In fact, I haven't had as much as a cold since 2010. Whenever a health condition threatens to come upon me, I remind my body who I belong to and that Jesus died for my complete deliverance and healing. I also do not give a foothold to the devil; I don't give him legal access to my body through disobedience. Just because I'm healed doesn't mean I can do whatever I want to do. I will not cheapen God's grace because I can't control my appetites and my cravings. Because He's done so much for me, I will do my part to thank Him through obedience.

If God is calling you to a certain diet plan, just do it! The struggle is real, but you have a power in you that is bigger than the struggle and bigger than any food challenge you are facing. Don't you know He loves you and wants the best for you? He isn't taking away the foods you love to punish you; He just knows that if you keep down that path it will destroy you and all that He has planned. Don't be a slave to your appetite. Don't be the author of your own demise. If I can change, so can you. I cried out to God and He changed my palette, He can do the same for you.

Even if it feels impossible right now, the minute you say yes with your heart, you'll invite grace to empower you. With that power you will be able to not only conquer your food demons, but all the other demons that threaten to overtake you, your family, your community and your nation. You are more than a conqueror, God has your back and He wants you well. Now it's time you do your part.

EXCUSES, EXCUSES, EXCUSES

Since changing my diet, I've heard my fair share of excuses for why people can't eat healthier. Over these years, however, I have developed quite the rebuttal for each and every one of them, especially the most common that are listed here:

"All in moderation." If I had a dollar for every time I heard people say they can eat sugary items as long as it's in moderation, I would be filthy rich. Often when I probe a bit, I find out that moderation rarely, if ever works for them. Trying to get deliverance from sugar, while still consuming it, is like trying to be free from crack addiction while still hanging out at the crack house. Imagine if you heard a drug addict say, "I'm only going to do cocaine once a week. It's all about moderation." You would think that was absurd. You should be equally repealed by the idea of sugar in moderation. Sugar is just as, if not more addictive in nature, than cocaine. There is research to support this idea. There is also no mechanism in the brain to shut off sugar consumption. Try as you might, moderation of white, refined sugar is a man idea. Seek God and ask Him what you should do about sugar. If you are a current sugar addict, let me know if He endorses the moderation philosophy.

"Eating healthy is too expensive." I used to think the same way, but if you think healthy foods are expensive try having an illness. Just one of the three cancer treatments I was administered was $5000. I had 6 rounds of that drug. That's $30,000. of which I had to pay $2000. That figure doesn't include my other out-of-pocket cost for child care, time off from work, gas, and wear and tear on my car. Nor the emotional cost of having a disease like cancer. In comparison, I would say eating healthier is worth every penny. My friend Karen says, "Pay me now or pay me later." I'll rather pay now and reap the harvest of my prevention.

Speaking of the emotional toll of cancer, I was kicked out of chemo for not paying my bill on time. This is a true story. At the 4th round of my chemotherapy sessions I was kindly informed by the women at the front desk that if I didn't pay my bill that day, I would be denied treatment. I informed her that an agency in New York was mailing a payment for the balance (our bills were piling up so fast we sought payment help). That wasn't good enough. I was kindly told to find treatment elsewhere. I cried all the way home. I did find an alternative site for chemo, but the damage had already been done.

When I first started eating healthy, I would complain to anyone who would listen. "Can you believe the price of this organic apple?" "I can't believe the cost of my groceries has nearly doubled since eating healthier." One day in the grocery line, just as I was about to complain to the person in front of me, the Holy Spirit whispered, "What are you complaining about? I've given you the money to pay for it." That truth stopped my complaining in its tracks. God says He will supply all our needs according to His riches in glory. God knows you need to eat right, so if you ask, He'll provide the way for you to do so.

I also came to understand that the healthier foods cost more because...they are food. The other items you are eating in the middle of the grocery store are nicely packaged science experiments. Have you read the ingredients? You probably can't pronounce most of them. I say if you don't recognize the word on the ingredients list, nor will your body.

"I don't buy fruits and vegetables because they spoil." This makes sense because that is what happens when produce isn't eaten, it spoils. The key here is to eat the produce that you purchase. If fresh is a problem, consider buying its frozen counterpart. Do what works for you.

"Fast food is cheaper and more convenient." This is true if you are looking at this from the short-sightedness that our microwave generation adheres to. But if you consider the long-term effects of eating items that are not really food at all, the costs are far greater than you ever considered. Sadly, the convenience of fast food gives way to a whole host of medical and emotional problems that are expensive beyond measure. Remember, "Pay me now or pay me later?"

Also, have you considered that fast food is not food at all? Have you ever cleaned out your car and found an old McDonald's French fry under the seat? If not, I have and it looked the same as it did the day I purchased it. That's scary to think I willingly put something in my body that doesn't spoil. Food that brings life spoils, so that must mean that food that doesn't spoil brings death. Nibble on that awhile.

HAS ANY SEEN JOSEPH'S SISTER?

You may be thinking, *great now that I know how to curb my natural desire to overeat, how do I also satisfy my emotional hunger?* I am glad you asked because I've been there.

The rejection I experienced as a child not only led me to overeat, but it also produced an emotional hunger in me for acceptance, belonging and love that no amount of food could fill. So, I sought to satisfy this hunger through the praises of men. Sadly, I desired that just as much, if not more than I desired God's approval. I needed to hear from people how great my talk was, or I constantly checked my social media posts for follower engagement, and longed to hear my name mentioned in acknowledgements at church or other organizational events. These praises from men were my lifeline; they fed my malnourished soul.

During this time period, God sent prophet after prophet to foreshadow His plans for my life. One Sunday after church, a woman I didn't know came up to me to tell me that God said, "You have no idea where I am taking you, I see Hong Kong, I see Asia, I see the UK." Another woman outside of a 7-Eleven convenience store said, "This thing you are doing is going to be so big. You will be a household name bigger than Joyce Meyers." Yet another prophet in Pittsburgh said, "I see you at a large circular table with Kings and heads of states and I see Oprah there too." Let's stop right here and pause for the Oprah Winfrey prophecy. That was a glorious day. My brother in Christ prophesied that word just months before I was to move to Chicago. I knew my time had come; Oprah and I were going to be best buds! To my horror, the year I lived in Chicago, I couldn't as much as get tickets to her show.

What was God waiting on? Didn't He hear what was said about my glorious future? Of course He did, but He wasn't in a rush. He was more invested in building my character, than my platform. He was and still is more invested in advancing His Kingdom agenda, then feeding my ego. So why had God's plan tarried? Not to torture me, but to give me time to learn to be fed by Him and Him alone.

God is not interested in executing His plans as a way for us to feed our emotional voids or our pride. He would rather we nearly starve then be fed in a way that would destroy us. Have you seen ministers that get out of the gate to early? Moving rapidly to a place their character can't keep them? It's not pretty.

Ironically, though I wanted fame for the shallow benefits of fame, I had enough sense to ask God to close the doors that were not for me and He did. Even with that I have pursued doors that were shut and now live to tell the horrid story. I recall one such opportunity, a speaking engagement I wanted desperately thinking it would finally get me out of "prison." Yes, after so many near-fame misses I started calling myself Joseph. Like Joseph, the *cupbearer* kept forgetting to tell Pharaoh I could interpret dreams! So, if he wasn't going to help me get out of prison, I was determined to make my own way out.

The host of the event I wanted to be a speaker for kept ignoring my attempts to connect. I would reach out, only to get zero acknowledgement or a lame, "let's connect next week." In error, I pursued that opportunity until the person finally said yes. To my shock, it was one of the worst experiences I've had as a speaker; it almost turned me against ministry.

From that point on I've learned, when the door shuts, unless God opens it, I am running the other way. If it's not for me, I don't want it.

It's taken a while to get here, but I've finally gotten to a place where the people mean more than the promise; where the promise is not bigger than the promise-giver; and where I only want to make His name famous.

I'm in this place of peace because God lovingly starved my need to be fed by men. It's been a long, arduous starvation process, but it has been worth every moment. Now I can honestly say I am no longer in a rush. God's timing is perfect, and if I never become a household name, I am okay with that. As long as I do what is pleasing to the Lord that is all that matters. I don't want to get to Heaven's gates and hear my Savior say, "You had a lot of Facebook likes, your followers on Instagram exceeded a million, you spoke all over the world, but I know you not." Rather, I am living to hear Him say, "Well done my good and faithful servant enter into the joy of the Lord."

God has covered me over the years; kept me from moving too fast, and perhaps He's doing the same with you. He wants you to succeed, but He can't bring forth your success until He has done a work in you. If the praises of men mean more to you than it should, meditate on Jeremiah 17:5-8:

> "Cursed is the man who trusts in man
> And makes flesh his strength,
> Whose heart departs from the Lord.

For he shall be like a shrub in the desert,
And shall not see when good comes,
But shall inhabit the parched places in the wilderness,
In a salt land which is not inhabited.
"Blessed is the man who trusts in the Lord,
And whose hope is the Lord.
For he shall be like a tree planted by the waters,
Which spreads out its roots by the river,
And will not fear when heat comes;
But its leaf will be green,
And will not be anxious in the year of drought,
Nor will cease from yielding fruit.

Let God fill you up; let Him feed your empty emotional spaces. Then and only then will you produce the fruit that will save this generation and be a light to a dying world.

PERSONAL REFLECTIONS

1. *Review the definitions that Dr. Celeste gave for appetite. Would you say you are a slave to your appetite? Which foods do you find challenging to eliminate from your diet? How has this food item(s) affected your health? Has this food been used to fill emotional voids? What emotions are you feeding?*

_____

_____

_____

_____

_____

_____

_____

_____

_____

_____

_____

_____

_____

_____

_____

_____

_____

2. As mentioned, Joyce Meyer claims to be disciplined in what she eats. How do you think she has gotten to a place of discipline and submission? If discipline is a challenge for you, what do you need to do to exercise discipline in your life? What new habits do you need to put in place on a daily basis?

3. It's time to take back your health. Have you played the "family history" card? If yes, has this mindset helped you or hurt you? What is God calling you to do in your health? Will you do it? Why or why not?

4. *What excuses are you making for not eating right? Based on what Dr. Celeste wrote about excuses, refute your excuses in your journal.*

5. *Dr. Celeste wanted success for some of the wrong reasons. God wants us all to succeed, but not at the expense of the call. Are you waiting on Godly success or are you anxiously pursuing any and every opportunity that comes along? If the latter, what emotion do you think is driving this behavior? What will you do to make peace with the pursuit of success at any cost?*

6. *If you are struggling with the approval of man, ask God to help you find freedom. Meditate on Jeremiah 17:5-8 and journal what the spirit speaks to you.*

CHAPTER 4

FREE INDEED

> "When you lose food as a friend, you may miss it at first; but soon you will see all the things it was taking away from you."
> —LAURA HOUSSAIN

Years ago, when the words "I've made peace with hunger," rolled off my tongue at a Starbucks with my friend Sundra and her son Jonathan, I knew I had crossed a threshold; I had entered a new dimension of His glory. How had I come to a place of peace with my physical hunger? By being filled with God's spiritual food: the Word.

Today, the Word has become better than my natural food. I no longer feel deprived, I no longer feel empty. Physical hunger, no longer triggers an inner longing. My inner longings no longer need to be fed by food. I have come to a place of peace, knowing that any hunger I face, whether natural, emotional, or spiritual can be fed by God.

I have learned to fully and completely depend on Him for my every need.

THE RIGHT KIND OF HUNGER

The Beatitudes of Matthew 5 are a series of eight blessings from Jesus such as, "Blessed are those who are poor in spirit for theirs is the Kingdom of Heaven." The fourth reads, "Blessed are those who hunger and thirst for righteousness, for they shall be filled."

Righteousness is defined as right standing with God. The scripture tells us blessed are those who long to be in right standing with God. He wants you totally devoted to Him. If food is a distraction from the issues you really should be addressing, asks God to give you the courage and the knowledge to deal with the real issues. Seek His face and His righteousness and finally make peace with hunger.

God has put an inconsolable longing for Him in our hearts that cannot be satisfied through anything or anyone but Him. Isaiah 55:2 reads, "Why do you spend money for what is not bread, and your wages for what does not satisfy? Listen carefully to Me, and eat what is good, and let your soul delight itself in abundance." Hunger and thirst are God-given desires, but He longs for you to satisfy them with His living water and His edifying bread. We all have an insatiable longing that can only be filled by Him.

Jesus has something to say about the insatiable hunger in your heart and the relentless thirst in your soul. His answer is found in Matthew 5:6. It is the human condition to be hungry; however, giving that condition over to the one who satisfies is our only hope for true fulfillment.

THE PROMISE

Exodus 20:2-3 reads, "I am the Lord your God, who brought you out of the land of Egypt, out of the house of bondage. You shall have no other gods before Me."

Victory can be found in this promise from God. He is the Lord your God capable of delivering you from any and every area of bondage, including the hold food has had on you. Your addiction to food started in Egypt, whatever your Egypt may have been, but as His child you are free. With His loving arm, He has brought you out of darkness, into His marvelous light. He is the father of lights and will shine His light on every dark area of your life and bring victory. In fact, victory belongs to Jesus and as joint heirs with Christ you are in turn victorious.

God declares in His word that He brought you out of Egypt. If you are a blood-washed believer, you have not only been brought out of Egypt, but Egypt no longer has to have a hold on you. Ask the Holy Spirit to change your mind. Indeed, when you change your mind, you change your season.

God also promised that when you are born of Him, you are a new creation; old things are passed away and behold all things are new (see 2 Corinthians 5:17). Even if food has a hold of you in such a way that you don't see a way out, it's not the truth about you. You are a new creation. If I could be delivered from the hold Egypt had on me, so can you. Remember, it's not the food that's the issue it's your connection to the food. When you break that connection/stronghold, through obedience and fasting, you will be free. Then you will see that what once held you bound no longer has the same effect.

It is said, "instead of telling God how big your problem is, tell your problem how big your God is." He's a great big God who brought deliverance to you through His son. Jesus not only died for your salvation, but that you might also find freedom in every area of your life.

PRACTICAL STEPS FOR FREEDOM

Acknowledge there is a problem. Dr. Phil McGraw says that acknowledgement brings you 50% of the way to solving the problem. The devil wants you to remain ignorant of his devices; he has used food to hold you bound. Shine your light on him and let him know you see him and his tricks and that you will no longer be a puppet for him to use. Take back your diet, your health, and your life.

Acknowledge you have sinned. As long as you pretend that "it's just food" you'll never recognize the need to change in this area. Instead repent and confess that you have made food your god. Repent means to turn and go in a different direction. Your repentance also represents your full reliance on God.

Remove all offending foods from your home. Be a participant in your miracle; set yourself up for success. If there are others in your home, share with them that you struggle with certain foods and you would prefer those foods to not be in the house for a while. If an adult insists on having the food in the house, ask that they hide it from you. This might sound radical, but as I was learning to master my food addictions, I had my husband hide the offending foods from me. I just never knew when the emotional craving for that particular food would hit me and I didn't want to sabotage my success from my own home.

If you have children and they are complaining, don't feel guilty. There was a time I ate well, but fed my family junk. One of my friends asked me point blank, why are you feeding your family food you know will kill them? I hadn't thought of it that way, but it made me think, *why was I allowing them to eat poorly by my hand?* Then it hit me, I didn't want to punish them with healthy foods. I still had an emotional attachment to the bad foods and didn't want my family to be deprived of the good feelings those foods once brought me. I was feeding them my past, but I was being called to make new food memories with those I loved. Now instead of using overly processed, fake food, I cook from scratch and feel good about feeding my family life.

I witnessed firsthand the fruit of my obedience in this area. From Pre-Kindergarten until 3rd grade, teachers told me time and time again my son AJ was too "active" in class. Having worked in the school system, I knew that was code for *your son has ADHD and needs to be medicated*. It's not that I don't believe ADHD is a real diagnosis, I'm just from the school of thought that it is over diagnosed, especially for our boys of color.

The summer before AJ was to enter the 3rd grade, I took sugary breakfast cereal out of his diet. When we met with the teacher at the first parent/teacher conference I was bracing myself; I was waiting for the teacher to announce that he was "too active." At the end of the teacher's feedback I tentatively asked, "Do you have a problem with him being too active in class?" He said, "No, why do you ask?" Andel and I were flabbergasted. I immediately knew taking sugar out of his morning breakfast lineup made all the difference.

My kids are allowed to have one sweet treat a week. Ironically, when I took the sugar out of their diet, I noticed them picking up unhealthy substitutes like more television. Now they can only watch television in the morning and on the weekends. It's amazing how making changes in your diet can open your eyes to other poor decisions and choices. How you do anything is how you do everything. Junky diet, junky life. Healthy diet, healthy life.

Be prepared for hunger. Until you become perfectly comfortable with physical hunger, keep a snack in your bag. Nothing will get you running back to Egypt faster than a hunger you are unprepared to tame. Keep healthy snacks with you so that stopping at a Fast Food restaurant is less appealing.

Thankfully as you grow in this area, you'll be able to tolerate your hunger pains. Now I can be hungry for hours (if circumstances dictate) and not grab an unhealthy snack. Mastering natural hunger has taught me patience, not only in diet, but other areas of my life. Now I can be hungry for an opportunity and not take the first good chance that comes in my path. I can also be hungry for something material, like a car and not act on that impulse. I've learned to wait on the Lord and be of good courage. It takes courage to allow yourself to go hungry, but I know that in due time, if I am patient, I will eat of His good works. His Word tells us that His people shall eat in plenty and never to put to shame; that is, if you are eating from His table. In other words, if you are obedient to what and when He wants you to eat, you will never be put to the shame of obesity, disease, humiliation, bankruptcy, sexual scandal or any other vices hunger desperation can lead to.

Declare today you are free; no longer bound, but whole in every way. Ready and able to do God's magnificent work and fulfill the call that is on your life.

DELICIOUS HEALTHY SNACKS

Developing a good healthy eating lifestyle is not just about what you take out of your diet, but also what you add in. There are plenty of items that you can add in that are easy and delicious; life is too short to not enjoy your food. The following is a list of snacks that are healthy and delicious.

Many of which I enjoy myself. You can google any of these snacks by name to find the recipe. Bon Appetit!

Savory Snacks

- Air-popped popcorn with coconut oil and balsamic vinegar
- Popcorners
- Cut vegetables with hummus
- Popchips
- Raw Nuts
- Seeds
- Roasted seaweed
- Roasted chickpeas
- Pita chips

Sweet Snacks

- Lily's Stevia Sweetened Chocolate Bar
- Apple slices with almond butter
- DIY Trail mix
- Dried fruit
- Oatmeal Cookie Energy Balls
- Baked apple chips
- Fruit smoothie
- Luna bars
- Clif Nut Butter Bar
- Granola

PERSONAL REFLECTIONS

1. *Reflect on Matthew 5:6, "Blessed are those who hunger and thirst for righteousness, for they shall be filled." What does this scripture mean to you?*

2. *Why do you think God puts in our hearts a hunger for Him?*

3. *It's important to be proactive when making changes. Are you worried about the way your dietary changes will affect others? If you have a family will you implement the changes that you are making onto them? Why or why not?*

4. *One key to success in the area of diet is preparation. How will you need to prepare for each day so that you not sabotage your success? Make a list of healthy snacks that you can take with you on the go. Download an app like Clean Plates that tells you the healthy restaurants in your area. If you have gone gluten-free, download the app Find Me Gluten Free. If you're vegan, try the app Happy Cow. There's plenty of help on the internet, use it!*

CONCLUSION

Two behaviors allowed me to arrive at my place of healing: honesty and obedience. I have had to surrender my agenda, my rights, and my free-will to God so that He could heal me from the inside, out. Surrender is doing God's will, His way. If you are going to be "free indeed" you are going to need to listen, acknowledge the truth and obey.

From my first Surrender Fast from food God started me on a journey to wholeness that has ended in my total wellness spirit, soul, and body. Am I perfect? No. Do I sometimes mess up with my eating? Absolutely. However, the key to sustaining success is not to focus on perfection, but focus on Him. God is not calling us to be perfect, He is just seeking to use those who have a heart that is perfect towards Him.

I'm no different from you. I've been successful in this area only because of His grace. All along the way I've been honest with myself and God, and obedient to His instructions. I stopped pretending that my addiction was no big deal and I stopped making excuses. Now I am able to go in His flow and travel at the speed of God in every area of my life. Let surrender advance you as it did me. It started with food, but it ends with Him. And He has brought me to a place of peace with hunger.

ABOUT THE AUTHOR

D r. Celeste Owens is a sought-after international speaker and facilitator whose mission is to equip people to live free and whole through the surrender of spirit, mind, and body. A transformative healer, she uses the word of God and psychological principles to bring others to total wellness.

Dr. Celeste and her husband, Andel co-founded Dr. Celeste Owens Ministries, an international healing ministry and travel the globe sharing the philosophy of surrender. They believe that when God is the center there is nothing one can't do!

Celeste knows all about surrender and its ability to advance. In 2009, in what she calls an Abraham moment God called her to leave all that she knew—private practice, public speaking, and ministry leadership. And in an act of radical obedience, she did. From that place of humility and surrender God birthed her first book *The 40-Day Surrender Fast*, a devotional designed to help the reader develop a more intimate relationship with God.

An accomplished scholar, Celeste holds a Bachelor of Arts in Psychology from the State University of New York at Buffalo, a Master of Science in Applied Counseling Psychology from the University of Baltimore and a Doctorate of Philosophy in Counseling Psychology from the University of Pittsburgh.

A 13-year Breast Cancer survivor, Celeste has personally experienced the advancing power of surrender. In 2010 she surrendered her diet to God and through the process of fasting adopted a clean-eating lifestyle. In fact, her personal battle with cancer inspired her to become a Certified Natural Health Professional. Now this once self-proclaimed "junk-food-junkie" is thriving post cancer and inspires others to do the same.

Dr. Celeste has graced many pulpits and stages including the First Baptist Church of Glenarden, Pastor John K. Jenkins, Sr. (Upper Marlboro, MD), The Latter Rain Cathedral, Pastor Donald Chisholm, Sr. (Lockport, NY), and Antioch Christian Fellowship, Bishop George Mamboleo (Nairobi, Kenya) and presented at many numerous conferences and retreats. She has been featured in Essence and Heart and Soul Magazines, the Washington Post and a television guest on Let's Pray! She's also a member of Delta Sigma Theta Sorority, Inc.

God has provided an opportunity for Celeste to meet both the spiritual and physical needs of the poor through her nonprofit organization, Surrender 365, Inc. the mission's arm of Dr. Celeste Owens Ministries. Surrender 365, Inc. helps people all over the world to develop a deeper relationship with God and experience the liberating power of surrender through the teaching and preaching of God's word.

Surrender 365, Inc. also facilitates the provision of critically-needed goods and services to the poor and needy. Surrender 365, Inc. is a registered business in Kenya (Africa) and the work continues through its various Certified Ambassadors.

Surrender is what Celeste does. She will continue to encourage others wherever she may go to do God's Will—His Way—All the Time!